GODS TRUE AND LIVING DAUGHTER

GODS TRUE AND LIVING DAUGHTER

CINDERELLA

iUniverse, Inc.
Bloomington

GODS TRUE AND LIVING DAUGHTER

iUniverse books may be ordered through booksellers or by contacting:

iUniverse
1663 Liberty Drive
Bloomington, IN 47403
www.iuniverse.com
1-800-Authors (1-800-288-4677)

ISBN: 978-1-4620-5538-8 (sc)
ISBN: 978-1-4620-5539-5 (ebk)

Printed in the United States of America

iUniverse rev. date: 09/19/2011

The Real Life Story of Gods True and Living Daughter

The Real Life Story of Jesus as His True Sister

The Real Life Story of Real Life Living As Jehovah's Servant

The Real Life Story as Cinderella

Now as for me Jehovah's daughter

This is the production of the real life of Jehovah's daughter.

How I became his true daughter started when I was about 16 years old. I had a vision one night that there was a bad storm coming it was black and trees all around the wind was blowing so hard, and there was a big girl and a big boy standing on a porch they were about 12 years old. I knew I had to get them to safety but I could only carry one at a time, so I picked up the big girl and when I did she turned into a baby in my arms a newborn.

I went running for the trees to get the baby to safety but there was a barb wire fence I couldn't get over, and this figure came down in front of me and said Cindy you don't have to get over the fence I will protect you and anybodies who with you at all times, when I turned around there were people and animals in this field and sunny as can be it was very peaceful.

All I knew growing up is that I wanted to take back what eve had done to God.

Right after that dream I became allergic to chicken and turkey and eggs. And another thing I have that girl a boy on that porch I have twins that's right a boy and a girl.

Satan has tried to take me out quite a few times or somebody I loved and Jehovah's has always intercepted.

Like a fire in my apartment right at the front door. But for some reason I would always pray to God if there was a fire by the front door how would we get out. Well we all found a way out that night. Me and my 8month old baby and my husband. That apartment was where I received my first bible, that I have given to Molly Pike which at the time became my best friend. I started telling her I was Gods true daughter. But we have lost touch.

Then there was a bad car wreck on Kipling rd. Why I didn't die was beyond me. My legs all buckled up car door wouldn't open. The stick shift my hand slid down it and I took off the rear view mirror with my head that's what stop me from going threw the windshield and my head platting against the tree right in front of me. So that's twice Satan tried to take me out, and with no luck mind you. Then when my twins were 3 yrs old and my other daughter 8 we moved in springwood village. I was fighting for abused children that I was babysitting, by the way their parents was the one doing the abusing. I had a breakdown that's when I was going to White Oak Christian Church with me and my children. I thought my boyfriend was going to kill me. I went into the hospital for 23 days I couldn't distinguish who was good or who was bad but I thought his dad was God and my dad was Satan. But I knew I had to turn in my dad to God even though I loved him dearly so I had him come to the hospital to see me. Nothing happened to him of course. So I thought there was going to be a fire on the floor I was on the whole floor was going to be on fire but it didn't there was just a little fire in the TVs. room but all the doors were shut and locked to all hallways.

When they found the medicine that worked for me I told them not to change it I felt like Cindy again.

Then when I got out, we moved to Snowflake lane. And the Jehovah's witnesses came to my house and I was waiting on them. I started going to meetings with them at their Kingdom Hall. That's when Jehovah told me I got sick because of their wine at White Oak Christian Church. Where also I told the minister their named David that I was Gods true daughter he just laughed at me. Now who has the last laugh?

Then I got a job at the schools my kids attended Mt. Healthy. They wanted me to get a flew shot so I went to the doctor and the night before on the news said if anyone was allergic to eggs or yeast not to get the shot. So I ask the doctor the next day if it had eggs in it he said yes. That would have killed me if I had taken that shot. That's the Satan tried to kill me, one more time.

By the way, the breakdown I had was the black storm in my vision. Then one day I was praying to Jehovah God that I wanted to be the most beautiful flower to him opening up like flowers do when they are blooming. And this little girl name was Amber Hindman that was my daughter's friend brought over these beautiful pink fluffy flowers right before I was going to my meeting that night. That answered my prayer that day about being the most beautiful flower to Jehovah God that day.

So I have been collecting them ever since, they are little glass knickknacks, with little pick flowers on them. So on another night there was a star in the sky and I was taking Tracy Kinney home that night, and this star looked liked it was a puppet on a string. When I would turn right it would turn right when I would turn left it would turn left when I went straight it went straight, until I came back home and told my daughter to take Tracy back home so I can go in and take a bubble bath and they said the star came all the way down to the ground when Kimberly left. Tracy was so amazed that night and so was my daughter but I said it was Jehovah God doing this.

So as my life continued on with my ex boyfriend I thought I would die every night I went to bed with my twins laying next to me Gregory 2 and Kristina. Gregory on one side of Kristina and me on the other side. At night I thought my ex boyfriend was going to slit my throat he hated Jehovah God the most. I would see Satan come threw him daily as he would spit on me or push me or say something like do you think Jehovah's going to take care of you I would stand up to him and say yes he will.

I used to have a friend or what I thought was a friend who lived nearby her name was Dee but to find out she really was no friend at all. No matter what I wanted I would tell her she would go out and buy it for herself. Then when I finally got my divorce she left her husband and made a move for my new husband by trying to kiss him right in front of me. That was it that was the last time I saw her.

Then one Sunday I went to a meeting at the Kingdom Hall and Jehovah did a talk on a conversation that Beverly Rainy And I had the day before on the phone we both cried. She was the one who brought me into the truth by studying with me every week. Then they disfellowed shipped her for smoking and that made me so mad that wrote the brothers in New York City about this and that I was Jehovah's true daughter and they never wrote me back at all. You see it's not what goes inside you that makes you bad it's what comes out of you that makes you bad that means what comes out of your heart. Because we all have weaknesses.

I tried to tell the brothers this and about how Jehovah raised me on children movies such as Cinderella, Mulan, Pocahantic, Simba 2nd, and the movie called the Seeker. And also I like Harry Potter a lot. Cinderella was made for me because of my wicked stepmother and sister that I just found out was my sister and not my cousin about 8 years ago.

Jesus said he also came to save the world and not to destroy it like everybody thinks. But if you do not listen to me and what I say about Jehovah God and Jesus you will also be destroyed by them. Because Jehovah told me no matter what Satan uses against me it will not harm my children or me.

That means anybody who is on my side will not be destroyed also. Satan just tried once again to take my husband from me with meningitis from a cold the day before. And also a very good friend that I gave medicine to help him with his back and tried to kill himself that night he survived also. I love him to death but I would of went to jail for giving him medicine to help him.

See Jehovah is still watching my back even though I didn't do anything to hurt any body Now that I've gotten older Jehovah put out a new movie for me because I wasn't for sure about what I should do and the movie is the DaVinci Code. Where she is the female they have all been looking for Which that girl is I

Would give you Everlasting Life in his Kingdom, right here On earth. He said the righteous will inherit the earth and

Thank You Father for allowing me to write about you And being the true daughter of the one True God.

About Life and Death Would give you Everlasting Life in his Kingdom, right here On earth. He said the righteous will inherit the earth and The wicked would be destroyed. That in the book of Psalms. He has given me life with my children and grandchildren. These are Jehovah's grandchildren and great grandchildren.

Now Death is a different story. Jesus said of the dead that Thank You Father for allowing me to write about you And being the true daughter of the one True God.

About Life and Death wicked would be destroyed. That in the book of Psalms.

He has given me life with my children and grandchildren. These are Jehovah's grandchildren and great grandchildren.

Now Death is a different story. Jesus said of the dead that life is very good as long as you are serving Jehovah God And his son Jesus Christ our Savior and Lord. He said they are sleeping in Leviticus it says there is no work or thoughts when you are dead. But one good thing is that those who have fallen asleep in death will be resurrected Right here on earth. Instead of reading about the obituaries You will be reading about resurrections.

In Revelation 21:3 and 4 it says With that I heard a loud voice from the throne say "Look! The tent of God is with mankind and he will reside with them and they will be his peoples. And God himself will be with them.

and fantasies about them remember to get into the Kingdom Of God we have to be like children that what Jesus said here on earth. And about Jehovah God he is the one writing everything I've written in this book all of his thoughts not Mine his. He knows how to get things done, as we need to.

And about my past please forgive me father for everything I've done and still do. I love you Father like no other and your son Jesus Christ our Savior and our Lord.

Thank You Father for allowing me to write about you
And being the true daughter of the one True God.

And he will wipe out every tear from their eyes, and death will be no more, neither will mourning nor outcry nor pain ve anymore. The former things have passed away.

And the One seated on the throne said: Look! I am making all things new. Also, he says "write because these words are faithful and true." And he said to me: they have come to pass! I am the Alpha and the Omega the beginning and the end.

Also after these things I saw and look! a great crowd, which no man was able to number, out of all nations and tribes and peoples and tongues, standing before the throne and before the Lamb, dressed in white robes; and there were palm branches in their hands.

And they keep on crying with a loud voice, saying Salvation we owe to our God who is seated on the throne and to the Lamb. Revelation 7: 9-10

I love you Jehovah with all of my mind, heart, soul, and strength. Love you Cynthia K. Begley ii

To Jehovah my Father I come before your Throne

Through my Reigning King and High Priest Jesus Christ my Savior and Lord'

My Father Jehovah, please let your name be sanctified and your will take place on earth as it tis in Heaven. To Jesus Christ My Savior and Lord.

I know you are finishing my training, but I know you said your people did not have understanding, Please give them understanding, since you are King and High Priest.

To The Anointed

Jesus said of the Transfiguration that means he does also what the Father does. Well he has trained me since I was born always by directing my heart with choices but my flesh was weak. He showed me that Moses a leader and miracles, and Jesus his True Son and King, and Elijah a Prophet, that ail of these would be in one, but the Transfiguration is a female with all of these qualities, and if he would of put out in his magazines or only what he wanted you's to know then any female could come forward but since it is a secret until now its time and I know I'm probably the only one that has written you like it. A secret could only be between 3 people, Jesus, Jehovah, and I. He says nobody knows what's in store for them. Jesus is in the midst of his enemies, now its time to clean up my Father stepped in 12-17-98. This is Ezekiel 12;28 There for say to them, This is what the Sovereign Lord Jehovah has said;
There will be no postponement anymore as to any words

When You Go Before My
Father at Judgment

Humble yourself in spirit and bow,

Go before his throne and do not be to Proud;

He remembers the good you do, when you do it out of love, humble yourself before my Father and he will forgive you through his Son:

He takes you back spiritually, as a child 16:
He gives you lots of bubble baths, as he smiles proud:

He puts out a new song of Love almost everyday, (He says listen) I come in all forms and this is one way:

I went through this a couple of days, it was the greatest feelings I'll show you the way:

Then I grew up about 17 then 20, this was a big event I was with a baby and had plenty:

I turned 22 yrs. old then I was single, I met a boy who I do love and married him for 16 years, and he threw it out, just like an old jingle:

Then he took to me to 25 that's when I had twins, and is one of the best part of our lives and they began;

From then on, I became 38,the age I'm at now Jehovah makes everyday I want now to wake because He's Great:

He started this judgment of February 2nd, 1999 it still goes on and he granted me life,

You see I am just now becoming an adult; it took Moses, and Jesus the same time when they wrote:

The time frame of my Father differs from Yours, When you think of men and women at our times we are just children my Father adores:

To get into the kingdom of God you have to become like children, put your hearts into it and see the vision:

Please use your imagination of the children's movie (Hook) He saves the children right out of the book:

We have minds that are young, Even if we make it to 80, our bodies don't want to have fun: and this is done:

I am before my Fathers Throne Everyday, please bow our heads and let us pray:

To My Father Jehovah I come before your Throne in all our behalf, these are brothers, and sisters please don't let them pass, We are all colors, shapes, and personalities; these are all qualities that we need, please forgive us we are on our knees;

I ask all this through My Reigning King and High Priest Jesus

(Jesus Prayer)

My Father Please:

Let your Name—Jehovah be sanctified (or be made Holy) Please let your Kingdom come Your Will Take Place as in Heaven also upon Earth (Kingdom means government or ruler ship) He cleansed the Heavens in 1914 in October, of Satan and his Demons, and castled them down to earth:

1st world war and 2nd world war, Starvation, diseases: And so Jesus said Woe to Earth (Revelation) now he has to do it to Earth:

The meek and righteous will inherent the Earth: (Psalms) The wicked will be cut off:(Psalms) You see if you rent out a house to tenants and put ones who will keep it clean: Then you get rid of the old tenants and put ones who will keep it clean: This Earth is one of Jehovah's houses

Please give us our Bread and forgive us our Sins:

To be given daily Bread could mean: Spiritual plus physical Food: You need Physical Food for the physical Body to Live: You also need Spiritual Food to Live: You are a living Soul You have to feed the main organ the heart: You have to feed your heart with every word that is Truth can only come from Jehovah:
Spiritual Food is his word He will supply daily for your needs, if you don't eat everyday you will get sick:
Jehovah will forgive us our sins no matter how Great or Small if we can forgive each other and have mercy for one another and quit finding fault with each other: We all have faults or sins or debts they are all just different mine from yours or yours from mine: But Sin is sin and it all weighs the same:

If you want to be forgiven big, you must forgive, remember my (Father wants Mercy instead of judgment): Let your heart be drawn by love by my Father, He will truly show you what love is. (He does not take delight in death)

And lead us not into temptation and deliver us from the wicked ones:

Well when temptation comes up, we all fall short of the glory of God. But we do want him to deliver us from Satan and his demons: Now we don't want to recite these words there is allot of categories just in this prayer:

If you truly want love, talk to him just as you can see in the old days of going before Kings, on the movies but remember he is Love. Love does not hurt,

Thank you my father for this time that hopefully all our hearts will go to Love you more, and more, No End—(The Book Of Life)

You see there is no end to this prayer and the bible is the Never Ending Story, Life goes on and to who wants it freely, You Give Freely you will get Freely (You know what free means) you cannot make money off of this.

In Jesus Name I Pray Amen

Love you always Jehovah and his Son Jesus Christ

Love Cinderella

Thank You my Father Jehovah God And Our Reigning King and High Priest Jesus Christ

I wanted to write, to show you insight of the only True God and his Son, to show Jehovah's Power and Might:

The way you showed me growing up, since a little girl, you have showed me right and wrong, and all that stuff:

As Cinderella and Pooh, you called me by name, I know I'm your True Daughter, you told me so as we play games:

You like to play hide and seek with me, you would give me a clue, and I would study, read, and write, And act like the movies for children that you put in our sight:

You are beautiful, strong, and the Most Powerful True God I know You are Merciful, Gracious, and Kind, there is only one like you, that is your Son Jesus Christ:

I want to beg for Forgiveness and Mercy, I am very sorry for wanting to grow up in a hurry:

You've seen me do good and bad things, I never wanted to cover or ignore the sins I've accumulated, I just wanted to be perfect and clean, just one woman you could adore and enjoy:

I'm sorry what Eve Had done to your heart I have lots of feelings about this and you showed me she is very smart:

You are my best friend and you've been with me from the start, you've always have been loyal to me and I love you with all my heart:

I know you will turn it into a paradise, here on earth; we wait and wonder when you will step in and take our sides:

You are Willing, Wanting, and Capable, your ready to take your stand, because of our Love, and Faith, and we all beg for Mercy, and Forgiveness because you are the only one able:

I know you see and hear this, Thank You My Father, because you and your son I can't resist:

The Children's Movies watch, little Princess, Cinderella, Lion King 2 and Milan:

I Will Love You 4-Ever

Love Cinderella

Animals

Animals are so precious in Jehovah's eyes, look how many different sizes, and kinds that he created for our pleasure in our spare time:

If anybody hurts an animal at anytime my Father will see to it that you get caught and do time:

They are beautiful too, look at and touch, we don't just see in black and white, its colors we see to enjoy, and hands to feel the softness of all the furs of the animals even the ones that are just toys,

The food we get from animals, is a delight, you just don't eat out you can taste it and enjoy the flavor as you take a bite:

They are loveable, soft, and furry, quiet a few of them are people's children's or best friends, love the animals and the harmful kind of killings will end:

Be good to them they are Jehovah's pets, if you harm and innocent animal its a big offense:

Thank You Love
Cinderella

Cindy (Cinderella)

Meaning Moon Like the Moon up above You are constant and bright, wherever you go, you bring joy and delight,

Gifts my Father Has Given Me

My Father Jehovah sent me flowers,
One of the greatest times of my life he used his power,

My Father gave me a gift a bracelet that fit nicely, that had blue chips,

The long distance call to my dads cost lots of money, Jehovah changed the area code so we could talk and be lonely,

The bus stop was up the street and around the corner, my daughter began 9th grade and I began to be a worrier, before she started Jehovah changed the route, this bus picked up my daughter in front of the house.

These are a few things that my Father Jehovah took care of:

He says what I can't handle he will deal with it out of Love:

There is so much more I want to say: If you people put your heart into it My Father will show you the way:

Love Always Cinderella

Trust

I trust you Jehovah you're my Best Friend, down here Jehovah there is no trust, especially in any men:

Your Loyalty goes beyond what words could only tell you always talk to you and me straightforward never yell:

When you speak its soft and meek, I wait everyday on what you say:

If I turn right or left, maybe even fall, you grab onto my hand and you lift me up tall:

You always wipe my tears, since I was a little girl and all through my years:

You hold me oh so tight, I always asked you to, when I go to bed at night,

I trust you Jehovah with all my heart you have never let me down even from the start:

I rely on you, with everything I'm made have, I Would give you my life, and always being made fun of:

The pain from humans is so deep, the scar on my heart constantly day and night weeps:

I know you will wipe every tear from my eyes, I know you will give me another gift with a big surprise:

I need you now my Father like I never did before, you have drawn me so close to you, and you are the One True God I Adore:

Thank You MY Father Jehovah,
For Loving
Me now and always

: Love Cinderella

Faith

Faith is hope in every word my Father speaks, If you seek to please him He will show you, and you will become mild and meek:

Believe in all the things that's what my Father says, But don't be to gullible, its humans leading the way:

They speak, teach, and are imperfect; they all seem very confused looking for the right direction to take it:

Your name Jehovah means (causes to become) whatever I need you for, Even if I want to be young:

Faith in you saved my life, I wanted to give up especially at night:

I believe and write what you put in my heart and mind, you show me signs from heaven and you tell me I'll be just find:

The star the night it followed me, it looked like a puppet on a string, it went left to right in the sky, and it went backwards and forwards right before our eyes:

You gave me Faith in all forms I stood my ground for the One I Adore:

Sometimes doubt tries to come in, and then you tell me you'll always win:

I Fight and fight for your name, I'm ready to go against all who don't want to change:

I want them to know the Faith I Have, and I know soon in time you will take your stand:

Love always Cinderella

Loyalty

Loyalty, Loyalty, where did you go, I have lots of friends from years ago:

There are those who seem fake and those who are real; when they talk they seem to have no idea:

To understand their talk, walk, and how smart, Go to their level even if their a little tart:

Loyalty left years ago, when humans decided to take control, and did not want Jehovah's Rule:

Jehovah God is my Best friend; he will walk with me with eternity ahead:

I say, I will die for Jehovah; He says you will live another tomorrow:

He's there when I Call upon him, With Loyalty, Trust, and Faith, He believes in all of me, as his trust grows great:

Loyalty is one of the most things you need to have, and most people lost it and turned bad:

Love Always Cinderella

I BEG MY FATHER AND HIS SO JESUS CHRIST FOR MERCY AND FORGIVENESS

Jehovah god I am very, very, very sorry for writing down that I resign.

I want to stay in your favor and please always keep me by your side,

Please Father I beg you for my position back, where I was before in your eyes,

When I got Jealous and I didn't know if it was right or wrong and this is one way I do lack!

Those feelings I didn't understand you showed me and disciplined me

I know you reprove who you love, and its not fun

But you made my heart once again happy and glad.

I'm SORRY TO YOUR Son, Ijust got very confused and,

I know in my heart, I will love him forever and in my eyes he'll only be number one,

I'm SORRY YOUR MAJESTY, I DIDN'T mean to hurt yours or yours Fathers feelings, please pray to my Father and beg for mercy for me!

I just never really thought what I meant to you two, I'm

I'm down on my knees begging you please both your majesty

Please I veg please forgive me very deeply.

Jehovah you are my Best of best Friend, I will stay loyal to you

And your son as long as I LIVE and I still hope that means with Eternity ahead.

PLEASE KEEP TRAINING ME SO I CAN DO THE JOB RIGHT

Please keep watch over me and always hold me in your arms and walk hand in hand all day and night, I will listen and try to follow close by please never, ever let that thought enter in my mind, when I didn't think I was good enough for you and your son and made a decision and wanted to resign, Thank you for all the gifts.

And blessings you give, please don't stop tking care of my family and let us unite and always win!

The flowers you just handed me right now was threw a child, that says I'm forgiven and you are still very proud. Thank you my Father from the heart I have always wanted your approval from the start.

I KNOW I'm your moon flower and I thank, beg, I'm sorry

Through my Reigning King Jesus Christ with all of my heart

Thank you for forgiving me!

Lovwe alwaus, your little princess,your little girl from the start.

Friend,

Thank You
My
Father Jehovah,
For Loving me now
and always!
Love Always
and Forever
Mulan

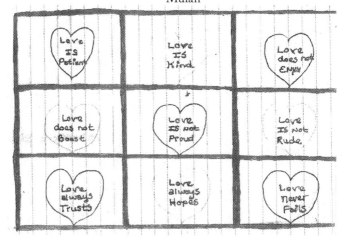

Thank You my Father Jehovah God And Our Reigning King and High Priest Jesus Christ

I wanted to write, to show you insight of the only True God and his Son, to show Jehovah's Power and Might:

The way you showed me growing up, since a little girl, you have showed me right and wrong, and all that stuff:

As Cinderella and Pooh, you called me by name, I know I'm your True Daughter, you told me so as we play games:

You like to play hide and seek with me, you would give me a clue, and I would study, read, and write, And act like the movies for children that you put in our sight:

You are beautiful, strong, and the Most Powerful True God I know You are Merciful, Gracious, and Kind, there is only one like you, that is your Son Jesus Christ:

I want to beg for Forgiveness and Mercy, I am very sorry for wanting to grow up in a hurry:

You've seen me do good and bad things, I never wanted to cover or ignore the sins I've accumulated, I just wanted to be perfect and clean, just one woman you could adore and enjoy:

I'm sorry what Eve Had done to your heart I have lots of feelings about this and you showed me she is very smart:

You are my best friend and you've been with me from the start, you've always have been loyal to me and I love you with all my heart:

I know you will turn it into a paradise, here on earth; we wait and wonder when you will step in and take our sides:

You are Willing, Wanting, and Capable, your ready to take your stand, because of our Love, and Faith, and we all beg for Mercy, and Forgiveness because you are the only one able:

I know you see and hear this, Thank You My Father, because you and your son I can't resist:

The Children's Movies watch, little Princess, Cinderella, Lion King 2 and Milan:

I Will Love You 4-Ever

Love Cinderella

Cynthia Kay Begley II

㉛

Thank you My Reigning King And High Priest Jesus Christ

I want to tell you a story, which once was a boy,
He grew up and became Gods True Son who we all
adore.

He is My Knight in Shining Armor,
He comes on a horse and he rides like no tomorrow.

I'm in Love with Jesus Christ,
He gave up everything for us, even his life.

You're kind, gentle, and handsome
I've always pictured you as our life's ransom.

There has been so much kindness on your part,
You are strong, powerful, and very smart.

The Love I have for you has grown,
It keeps getting deeper, and deeper,
So I don't want to be alone.

You are the light of my eyes,
If people could see what I see,
You would make our entire hearts cry.

The pain that you have suffered,
Makes me want to take back what is yours
Because we all stumbled

You're charming, witty, and intriguing
You're unique, humble and always believing.

I owe you my whole life, my heart goes
Out to you every night.

You are a hero, that we all have come to praise,
We thank you Jehovah's Son, and I want to
Show you in everyway.
I think about you night and day,
Theirs only one true love that can be,
I wish I could hold you, because you
Would show me the right way.
You mean everything to me, the stars
At night, look like your eyes that
Constantly sparkle bright.

Your hair is soft, clean and shinny,
And your body is tan, warm, and mighty.

I know that your voice is kind,
You are very well mannered, charming, and wise.

I'm very much in Love with you,
Please forgive me if my thoughts
And feelings are out of tune.

You would be the only one True Love
For me, there is nobody down here
That could compare or compete.

Thank you most Handsome Son,
For listening and hearing when my
Heart is full of laughter and fun.

I miss you Jesus Christ I need you with
All my might, I wish I had you in sight,
I would hug and kiss you and you would
Teach me everything right.

This is written to you, it's a love letter,
And I know you'll read it soon!!

Love you always
Cinderella-

Cynthia Kay Begley II

To My Only and One
True Love

I come before my only True Love I Adore,
You have me completely, from my head to my toes,
You are the only one man for me and the only one I won't
ignore,

You have become my best friend, Lover, Boyfriend
And I want you for my husband, and Please forgive me
For wanting to run away, now all I want is please never
leave me, please your majesty, and please always stay,

Your voice I do recognize it is so mild & meek & kind,
You are Tall Dark and Handsome, your beautiful Brown
Eyes, I see Trust, Loyalty, And Faith, Please teach me how
to give you my life as a Ransom,

The Pain that I feel for you what people had done
I won't let anyone touch you down here on earth, and I
will fight in anyway for you until Jehovah's work
Is done,

I will not let one Hair of your body be touched
In the wrong way by anyone,

I will give my life for you and to you until you
Get all the Love you Deserve, I know you gave your
For me, and I hope I can give it to you as a gift
In return,

You are the light of my life, and I will always
Follow you, if you turn left or right, backward,
Or forwards, I will always be behind you!

I want you to lead the way, the decisions you will make, I
Promise to you I will always stay and not stray,

I hope I can give to you a 100 percent, I might fall a whole
Lot, but I will try to be a better listener and make the long
trip,

I'm sorry when I make you mad,
I don't know when to shut up, and this makes me very sad,
I'm sorry I aggravate you with what I speak, I beg for
forgiveness
And I will try to watch my speech,

Right now I am very much afraid, when I hear
You get angry in your voice, I know you get very
Tired, I wish I could make you well and smile,

No matter what you do to me, I am very sorry
I know I deserve it all and now
I'm serious and this is not funny,

I don't know what to be for Gods True Son,
I really panic inside and want to run.

You are my True Love Elmer that finally came
I'm sorry for what I've done to you and very ashamed,

What ever it is my Father wants me to do all
I know is, I still want you unless my doesn't Approve!

                    Love always Cynthia
                    Begley II

Hope

Hope is all we have towards our Father, he says put hope in him
Like no other.

Hope is the wanting of something real bad and if you are good
in my Fathers Eyes he will make sure you get what you want
so you are not sad,

Hope is everything to us; think of him who gives all the stuff.

With out hope we are doomed, without hope all we would do
is be gloomed,

Hope is being in good health for life, and if you don't have
good health you just want to die,

Hope is waking up everyday and being able to see,
All the beautiful things out there even a bee sting.

Don't give up on Jehovah God put your hope and trust in him,
and he will give you what you want forever and always.

I am also going to get a divorce from my husband Elmer Ray Begley

He is not King any more because he was only King when we were married not no more it is totally over between us

And by the way he is still in Jail He went in to jail March 12 2009 and he will be in there for awhile. I am very sorry for him but it is totally over between us.

I am tired of getting hit it is over so whoever will be King that will be my choice and nobody else's. I do not think I will ever get married again.

I did love Elmer completely but it stops right here. Well that's how it goes I guess

Jehovah, I ♡ Thee

The #7 GOD IS,

Drew by a 13 yr old boy.

14/8

To MY Daughter Mulan and to her little Girl, My Grandchild Inside,

I Love you Kimberly Marie I don't know how to prove my love for you too see:

I would give everything I have to you, Especially True Love that you and that baby deserver from Timothy wanamaker the baby's daddy between you two.

I would give you Happiness and joy all the days of your lives I would take away the bad people say about you, cause you will be great:

Mother and wife and your my baby and you make my heart very, very proud:

I'm sorry for listening to what other people say you are a very good girl in everyway:

I wish I could become the mom you want me to be, I get very confused sometimes, but hopefully, my mind will straighten up and Elmer will teach me to see properly:

Their is a car that we will give to you I want other people to but out when it comes between me and you except for Elmer:

I wish others would have something nice to say about my children; I don't want to hear or you hear anything negative about you or T. J. Or the life you're given. 11 is everlasting life and you'll come off the winner:

I don't want anything bad to even come close to you or your family; I only want the Best for You with Life Everlasting:

I gave birth to you; you are one precious lady you will grow up always right, and I hope the gifts will be plenty:

If I could move to a great big house you would have your own wings for your Lives:

You will come to know Jehovah and Son, you will learn how real and precious they are and we don't have to run:

I want you to come and need me, I know I'll be there, I am coming all the way back and I'm not going to be scared I will love your family no matter who it is:

: Love you always and forever:

Your only and One True Mom

The Gift Of
Life Can
Only Come from
Jehovah God!

To My Daughter Poccahontas

You are my precious baby girl, you have been so wonderful and Beautiful all through your years:

I need you baby girl always by my side, I believe you that you tell me no lies,

I know what you've done and it was out of Love, I don't look down on you, I will put you above and that's true:

Your Gorgeous Blond Hair and big Blue Eyes, You are very rare and when you sing every body in for a big surprise:

I know you love Mom and I will never doubt you, I just don't want you to leave me, because I can't live without you too:

I will protect you from all that's out there; Please shoot Your Basket ball and they will go in for you:

You try, try and try so hard you will succeed at what ever you do:

You always do your best and that's all I expect you will always be MVP, to eternity:

I Love you my Daughter you are one great joy, I love the you are and you have a Twin that's a boy;

Don't give up, you will have the love of your Life, when your a full grown lady this will be nice:

You are my baby girl this will never you have a heart of gold and Jehovah will remove all chains,

I will try to be the Best mom you want Trust Jehovah and this is a Bonus also a Plus:

I Love You With All My Whole Heart from the start, I will Love you always unconditionally in all you do, I'll be here if need me too:

> Love Always and Forever
> Mom

The Gift Of
Life can
Only come from
Jehovah God!

Beauty

My first grandchild born
May 19th 2000

My little but, first granddaughter to be in our family. She is my first-born daughter.

She is 8 years old. Her birthday is May 19th 2000.

She is very special to me for one thing she is my first born, 2nd thing she looks just like her mother at her age she could have been her twin.

I had her the first three years of her life. Her mother was Pregnant with her son and other daughter and was very sick The whole time even thou Beauty could not handle the heat either. She loved to watch George of the Jungle sitting in her little Swing.

She is the most precious of all the grand children she was my first born of all the grandchildren. She sure does speak her mine about anything and everything that I like the most about her.

I love you Beauty you are grandma's first blessing from you Kim Carpenter.

From: grandma Cynthia K Begley.

To Tinkerbelle

Grandmas 3rd born

The baby
Born November 26 2003

Mariah you are just like my mom. There are no if buts about it. You are the sweetest most lovable child I had ever met.

You would go to any body and show them love that's how I know you got grandmas heart. So sensitive easily hurt.

Mariah when I see you I do see mom who I miss dearly but you are to young to stand.

You are Jehovah's great granddaughter isn't that a blessing come true.

To my precious little girl I will love you always and forever my baby Riri.

Love grandma forever and always
Cinderella

Simba 2
Born November 18th

My first granddaughter to my son. What day that was a blessing to see her when she was first born she was a-o.k.

She has grown up so beautifully she looks just like my son.

She knows grandma some because my son doesn't bring her around as much as I like.

She got blond curly hair and long. I sure do miss her. And the way she talks is clear it sounds like she is seven or eight year old talking. She will be with me soon as soon as this books goes out and my children don't think I'm wacko.

Love you Tianna
From grandma
Cinderella

Girls

Girls just want to have fun, with shopping and getting our nails done:

Our hormones go crazy growing up to maturity and were not sluts:

Their long hair and make up they try, We can watch the movies, and we usually cry:

Speak to us in a voice of mildness alot of girls growing up are afraid cause of shyness:

We want to tell how we feel inside, If you will just listen we will have nothing to hide:

We like to talk on the phone, we get bored easily, and don't like being alone:

We love to play dress up. sing, laugh, and dance, We love to be held at night with a little Romance:

Flowers, and bubble baths, plants and animals. those are the things we want to share with a beautiful horse in the stable:

Love Songs, Letters, and phone calls are better to say I Love You with all my heart, Being together in arms almost everyday is a start:

We like you to say (You look beautiful today), and mean every word that comes out of your mouth, Stop screaming and yelling or even a shout:

We want a little conversation, with your undivided attention, and your concentration:

We want Love instead of hate, call someone special and make a date:

We only want you to look at us the proper way, We might be a Bitch at times but with alot of trust, we're able to change are moods and our minds:

Hug and kiss us like never before, we only want one true love that we can adore:

We like games, sports, and cars, we read books at night until it gets dark:

Romance and kindness if you treat us with mildness, we will stand by men, that tell the truth, if your dishonest to us you get the boot:

Dresses, purses and shoes, girls get addicted to these things, and we like to sleep till noon:

All girls are my Fathers daughters, we are all really princesses and the women are going to be a large army

Jewelry, perfume, and candy, we like to look pretty, and we are very handy:
To take a drive at night, you see everything in the sky and Jehovah made things, pretty to the sight, as you hold each other tight:

To take us to dinner, or if you can cook, you look like a winner and not a jerk:

We want sex out of Love, if men can't look at the only one their with, then the relationship is done:

We don't like liars, and cheaters, this is not the way Tell us the truth and we will want to stay:

Girls can be everything nice, from sugar to candy with a little spice:

Sometimes girls get attitudes, we look in our hearts, and think whats wrong with you:

Our bodies go through alot of changes, from little girls to full grown ladies:

Try and try men to show us love we might be in adult bodies but our skin is as soft as doves:

We are all imperfect girls if you give us a chance, we will make this place a better world:

Girls are precious in Jehovah's eyes try to clean our hearts and put only Love inside:

My Father loves his little women, whether your short or tall or another color giving:

Our bodies mean alot to us, we exercise and diets we don't trust:

Girls are made very special, no matter what shapes and sizes, and Love beautiful weather:

We liked to be clean and tan, we want to wear bathing suits and play in the sand:

Girls are special and we don't want to lie, we tell Jehovah everything, because we don't need to hide our insides:

Women dream of having a baby one day, taking care of it if a family way:

The birth of a baby the pain can be severe, when you're in labor for hours it will bring tears:

Having a little girl at birth, she is so precious, as she grows up from a little squirt:

I love my daughters with all my heart you have been so precious to, from the start;

Love always Cinderella

Life

MvP To My Son The One I
Adore
Simba

You are my son, amere boy growing up,
I'm watching you turn into a man and you'll always
Have my love!

I want True Love for you when you grow up,
With everlasting life, and you are not a punk,

You are a very good, good little Boy,
My Heart is so proud of you,
You are my son that I won't ignore,

I'm sorry I always jump to conclusions,
I come at you sometimes in confusion,
I will try to believe what you say,
Instead of yelling, I will love you
A better way,

I hope you will always need me, with loyalty,
And trust and this is the way,
And I will show you this is the way,
And I will show you this is a must,

I want to wrestle & play with you my son,
You are getting so much stronger and this is getting fun!

I will be here to catch you if you fall, Please always
Tell mommy if something seems wrong,

You are my son I will protect you always, I will be
By your side,

> Love you always
> And Forever
> Love mom!

To my only grandson
Timothy John Wanamaker
Born April 29th 2001

You are my first-born grandson to me what a blessing you are.

With all the problems you were born with like being blind and not being able to walk that well. Jehovah's going to take all of them problems away just like your grandpa Elmer with his M.S..

Your blond hair that fits you so well and you will always be special to me. T.J. You are Jehovah's true grandson and don't ever forget that even when he makes you all better.

I love you T.J. forever mama's boy.

Love you Grandma

To Clint Antonio Pugh

He was a god sent to us. To me my daughter and my husband. He brought her out to see us any time she wanted To see us. He watches her at her job just like a body Guard.

You see she works at a gas station which could get robbed At any time. He is there day and night for her. That's a blessing in its self.

He is strong like an ox. The strength this man has is so remarkable. He carried our couch all by himself into our house.

He is so kind and very generous. I have come to know and love Antonio as one of my own children.

I love you Antonio no matter what color your skin is.

Love always Cinderella

Boys

Wrestling, climbing, roughness, and toughness wild little boys always trying to bluff us:

They Joke they laugh and grow up to be players, when they were sweet little boys that used to say their prayers:

If the boys would want to cry, they wouldn't dare because of men outside, that's why boys can't talk cause they hold it inside:

They are tender caring, and mamas little boys we watched them grow into men just to be Shipped to war:

We know you security, with a job, money, and toys, if you get rid of that macho attitude and listen, to my Father you will have all that and more:

Your bodies you'll always trying to build it doesn't matter what shape, sizes and colors as long as you learn how to feel instead:

Your feelings you always want to hide, kinds words for you to speak is hard for you to find:

Some are courage's, heroes, and not afraid and they usually get into some kind of mischief and choose the hard way:

You've been very smart, since a little tot watching you take bikes and stereos and trust apart
When you were a little boy always playing sports, cars wrestling and Nintendo, at night you would be come afraid of the dark, and always wanting me to hold you

I would hold you, we'd say our prayers you would say I love you mommy and forget our cares

Boys are so very special when you took into their eyes, they tell mommy everything, even if they get into trouble at times:

The heart of a boy seems very quiet: He talks to his buddies and wants to stay up all night.

They like to shaving cream you while you're a sleep, they throw cold water on you if you want to take a shower, and they laugh, as you scream

They only want respect you look at them as punks, and thugs and always being criticize for the way they dress.

Boys will be boys no matter how you look at it. stand by your sons, Love them and have fun, because when they become men they want to move out and split:

My little boy. is my only son I would never trade him m for another one

I cherish the ground that he walks on if he decides to run and falls: I will pick you up, and take care of your scrapes and cuts and kiss your booboo and write you letters from mom

Most boys want to be like their dads, they want to follow them and learn, if they treat their mother right it makes the son's heart glad:

If a boy wants to speak his heart, men tell you we don't do that so don't start:

If they cry there considered a wimp Please show your feelings inside, and growing-up you'll win and make that long trip:

You are my only son, the one I adore, and Jehovah blessed me with one special little boy:

You are growing up to be a man, the tears that come down my face watching you grow up hurts, me cause you are my baby you understand:

Grow up loyal and watch your speech there's allot of people That doesn't understand your young language when you speak,

I know you don't, mean to be disrespectful but when older ones don't treat you right you have to stand up for yourself and show them you need allot of respect cause your little:

I know you are good little boys you learn to fight, with your sisters or brothers, over toys:

All you need is somebody to hug, kiss, and hold you, Show you allot of attention and sometimes scold you:

You are one special young man as you are growing up try to understand:

My love is unconditional I might get mad once in a while when you get into trouble:

I love you my only son Please forgive me if sometimes I'm grouchy and have an attitude and don't have fun:

You are the best little boy a mom could want I'm writing this part with a seal of a big Kiss:

Love You Always Mom

Cynthia {Cinderella}

Meaning Moon

Like the moon up above
You are constant and bright

Where ever you go, you bring joy and delight,
You love to have fun just to sing, laugh or dance,

And you like nothing more than a little romance,
You're the type of person others want to know.

For no one can ignore your effervescent glow.

This is on a coffee cup that came from my father!
I'm the morning moon or DAUGHTER OF DARKNESS

AND THE SON [SUN] BOTH GIVE LIGH

WE ARE ILLUMINARIES IN THE BEGINNING

OF GENESIS

WHICH MEANS GENIUS

THE ONE

JESUS CHRIST, YOU ARE THE ONE
YOU KEPT ME GOING WHEN I WAS DONE
YOU GAVE ME STRENGTH, WHEN I WAS WEAR
IT IS YOUR WAY, THAT I MUST SEEK

JESUS CHRIST, I LOVE YOU
YOU SHOWED ME THINGS I NEVER KNEW
WHEN I WAS COLD, YOU BROUGHT THE SUN
JESUS CHRIST, YOU ARE THE ONE

JESUS CHRIST YOU GAVE ME LIFE,
YOU LET ME STAND WITHIN YOUR LIGHT
WHEN I WOULD CRAWL YOU HELPED ME RUN
JESUS CHRIST, YOU ARE THE ONE

JESUS CHRIST I LOVE YOUR WAYS
YOUR SUN SHINES THROUGH ON CLOUDY DAYS
YOU SHOWED ME BEAUTY WHEN I SEE NONE
JESUS CHRIST. YOU ARE THE ONE.

JESUS CHRIST YOU BROUGHT ME HOME,
YOU LET ME KNOW IM NOT ALONE
I NEEDED LOVE, YOU SAVE ME SOME
JESUS CHRIST, YOU ARE THE ONE

JESUS CHRIST, I DO HAVE FAITH
WHEN DEATH IS NEAR, THEN DEATH I FACE
I'LL WALK WITH YOU, INTO THE SUN
JESUS CHRIST, YOU ARE THE ONE

JESUS CHRIST, I THANK YOU LORD
YOU CARRIED ME RIGHT THROUGH YOUR DOOR
AND NOW I KNOW YOU ARE THE ONE
JESUS CHRIST, OH BLESSED SON

Family

Take one day at a time to call on Family, the phone call you retrieve might come in handy:

We all need somebody everyday, we are physical people and Loves the only way:

Parents, children, and teens, need one day off through the week:

Their will be no working weekends, this is Family time, and we all need this time to spend:

You get on Friday a 2 day supply of whatever it is you need, it will be by your side:

Have fun, sing, and dance, Play a lot of Love Songs, and try to forget your past

We will all stay at our jobs, and work for free, we won't need any money, because we will all have what we need (for free):

Everybody can go to stores and get what we want, it will be Free, enjoy your lunch:

You can all live for a change, Instead of dying, we can get out of these chains that are binding:

My Father says: this is all true, Believe in him, and he will show you too:

The truth will set you free, from money, that brings slavery, The time spent worrying about money; You will bow down and Thank You Father (Please)

Spend family time and you will see your children grow, if you won't leave them you will gain their trust and their feelings will show:

A mothers job is 24 hours a day, I know sometimes you want to be by yourself, Instead, you tell the children you will stay:

You give of yourself all day long, you just want somebody to care, so you don't raise your children wrong, because a lot of people talk about you and stare, You talk and talk, till your blue in the face, but after awhile your children win the race:

Watch over them at least until they are 25, That's the age for them to grow up on the inside, and starts to decide:

A mothers work at home is one most important job, Her children always come first, With manners, morals, and even when they sob:

A dads job goes on everyday making sure his family is taking care of in any way:

He leaves in the morning, doesn't come home till night, He helps cooks and cleans, and loves his wife:

The support you give in mildness of talk, makes your family love you dearly,: Dad can we go for a walk:

The children that respects their parents will talk to them as humans, and not as little things with no merits:

Children obey Mom and Dad and Jehovah will bless you, with a heart not sad, but glad:

You will wake up in the morning to go to school, to read and write and how to live too:

Behave in school, this is the way, If you want to cause trouble, You will be disciplined, this no fun to say:

The Kingdom is for children, they are all Jehovah's babies and they will learn to start living, In a respectable and proper way:

Parents be patient you don't want your children to leave angrily or sad, or follow Satan:

These children are a blessing from my Father, take care of them, and you will prosper:

> To MY Children
> Love Mom

In the Name of Jehovah God and his son Jesus Christ our Savior and lord.

Today is 5-20-2009 my granddaughter birthday was yesterday May 19 2009 Oh how very Precious she is her name is Beauty at 9 years old so amazing She is Oh so very beautiful in her own little way. And I have a beautiful little girl here with Me also and her name is Casondra DeAnn Boelleke she is 2 years old and she calls me mama Cindy And she says it so cute. So far in my life I have had ups and downs like for instance my husband Elmer Ray Begley II is in jail for beating me up. IT hurt me so bad to have to call the police that day and also The day before was when it really started which was March 112009 and kept going till

March 12 2009 My body got very beat up bad enough I had to go to the hospital that's how Bad my body felt. Cause now a days I would have to be half dead to go to a hospital. By the way I have 3 Fantastic Doctors in all of the world for all I am concerned one Doctor is Name Doctor Nasseff he is a Pain management doctor which he doesn't just throw medicine at your or just take your money He really is a very special Doctor he sends you for all kinds of test he is the best Doctor because I am on The right medicine for me that helps me all the way with the pain I get in when I do not have any And that truly sucks because of withdraw it is a total witch that hurts the most so you better have

Your prescription for the end of the month and do not run out. But this Doctor is so kind even thou he has a different accent he is so awesome and I know he is going to be one Doctor who is going to heal

Any body he comes in contact with that what my father Jehovah says I do not know when Or how but it will happens because my Father Jehovah what he says goes out and will Not return to him until what he needs gets done . . . . So you can believe it is going to happen And this Doctor deserve everything but how well he treats you like a human.

I Come to you in the name
of Jesus Christ our Lord
and Savior

Father there is another Doctor called Doctor Desilva a fantastic Doctor as a psychiatrist he is a dam good doctor he talks to you even about god he listens and helps you with your problems also. And he also does not give out medicine just to give it out either and he knows exactly what you need when you need it it is so exquisite i just love him also just like I do Doctor Nasseff and Doctor Robles now here is a doctor with style and so kind and so smart at her jobs she takes care of you right away as soon as you need it then you might sit 10 minutes at the most in her office and she will talk to you like a human being also. and so very kind and very lovable she will to one day healing people also she just will and this is coming from Jehovah God Himself that you know it is going to happen to her also. Well I do love everyone of you Doctors very much and thank you for being so kind to me thank you Cynthia Kay Begley

I Humbly come before your Throne Jehovah God threw my Reigning King and High Priest Jesus Christ my Savior and Lord

Well this is the end of this Book and the name of my 2nd book is called The Good The Bad and the Ugly what a name and it is what it says it is. For instance the good will stand for the book of Good

Life and the bad stand for the wicked and the ugly stand for those who will get a 2nd chance at life if they truly want that. Or they can be destroyed again which this time is for you it is called the 2nd death in the back part of the Bible in Revelation and there is no coming back after the 2nd Death. You are gone and destroyed forever no life at all. i surely do not want that for anyone. I want life for all whoever wants it. Those who not and try to harm me or my family that includes people who are just friends for me. These people are under my protection so Satan stay the Hell away from every single person I love. Come and get me you piece of shit because I have Jehovah and his Son Jesus Christ my Savior and Lord and please excuse my language if I have offended you somehow. But I mean everything I say. I am not afraid of you because of a blink in Jehovah eyes you are and will be destroyed for a thousand of years then just for a little while you will be left out then gone forever. Jehovah is my Father and my Husband and Jesus is my Son and my Brother as well. We are Blood and there is a bloodline between them and me. You are wondering why I say I am Jehovah wife it is said that in the Book of Isaiah # 62 1-12 I also still his Daughter do not forget because he created me So I am his True and living Daughter and Wife the Scriptures explain every word that I say is true And the Scriptures that I am writing are from Jehovah God himself like for instance Isaiah #65 17-19 then 21-25 54 3-17 # 55 1,3,6, # 56 1,8, #57 4,14,19/ #58 8,9,11,14 # 59 1,3,4,6,7, # 59 18,19,21, # 60 1,4,11113,14, #61 1,6, 7,8,9,10 # 62 1, 2, 3, 4, 5, 6, # 62 1,2,3, 4, 5, 6, 9,10,11,12, #63 7,8,9, #64 8,9, These are just a few that you can look up to prove myself true to you people What I Speak it is my Father talking for me its not me its my Father Jehovah God.

Well this is the last piece of this book So I hope that you believe me because trust me you do not want to hurt Jehovah's Family down here because he knows what you are going to do before you do it. I love you my Father and Thank you for letting write about you

Thank You
Cinderella

This is about an awful good lady that I know

She is such a kind and loving lady who getting the raw end of the deal. She is supposes to go to jail sometime soon over child support this is not fair at all when she is working her but off to take care of her family at home making only 70.00 dollars a day That's very hard to do and then not getting appreciated for it that hurts and having a broken heart at the same time if it wasn't for her and her son they are the ones that save me from my husband that night when he beat the hell out of me. She reminds me of myself when I was 10 years younger mad as hell at the world and did not know how to fix it but I do now.

She is so very beautiful and a very close friend to me. Her son is gorgeous to and he is 17 and she is a Princess and her son is a real Prince to me I do love her beautiful daughter and her other son he is one handsome little boy and a very good boy at that. And her daughter is such a beauty just like her mom and all I pray for for her is hang on very soon you will have the life you deserve and wish for I Love all of yours Take good care of each other and love one another.

Love Always
Cinderella